Sports
for All

WELDON OWEN PTY LTD

Chairman: John Owen
Publisher: Sheena Coupe
Associate Publisher: Lynn Humphries
Managing Editor: Helen Bateman
Design Concept: Sue Rawkins
Senior Designer: Kylie Mulquin
Production Manager: Caroline Webber
Production Assistant: Kylie Lawson

Text: Robert Coupe
Consultant: Murray Phillips, Senior Lecturer in Sports Studies,
University of South Australia

04 03 02 01 00 99
10 9 8 7 6 5 4 3 2 1

Published in New Zealand by Shortland Publications,
2B Cawley Street, Ellerslie, Auckland.
Published in the United Kingdom by Kingscourt Publishing Limited,
P.O. Box 1427, Freepost, London W6 9BR.
Published in Australia by Shortland–Mimosa,
8 Yarra Street, Hawthorn, Victoria 3122.

Printed in Australia.
ISBN: 0-7699-0523-4

CONTENTS

Early Olympic Games 4

Shooting Arrows 6

On Track and Field 8

Fast Riders 10

Riding Horses 12

Gymnastics 14

Skating on Ice 16

In the Snow 18

Warlike Games 20

On the Water 22

Surf and Sea 24

Diving In 26

Under Sail 28

Glossary 30

Index 31

EARLY OLYMPIC GAMES

The first Olympic Games of modern times took place in 1896. They were named after a games festival held by the ancient Greeks every four years at Olympia. Only men competed in the ancient Olympic Games—there were separate games for women. Discus throwing, as shown here, was one of the events in the ancient games, and is also an event in the modern Olympics.

Horse Races
Chariot races and bareback horse racing were exciting and dangerous events in the ancient Olympics.

Foot soldiers in ancient Greece were called hoplites. In the hoplite race in the ancient Olympics, runners had to race each other while carrying heavy shields and wearing armour on their head and legs.

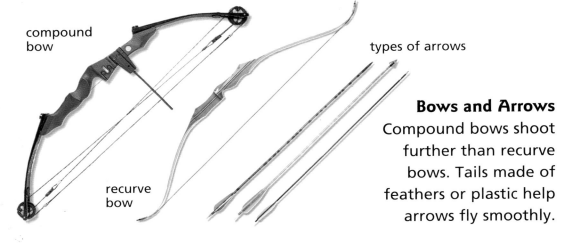

compound
bow

recurve
bow

types of arrows

Bows and Arrows
Compound bows shoot
further than recurve
bows. Tails made of
feathers or plastic help
arrows fly smoothly.

SHOOTING ARROWS

People who shoot at targets with bows
and arrows are called archers, and
their sport is called archery. Hundreds
of years ago, before guns were
invented, soldiers used bows and arrows
in battle. Here is an archery contest in
England about 200 years ago. At that
time archery was a popular sport
among wealthy men and women.

Bull's-eye
An archer
wins points
by hitting the
bull's-eye at
the centre circle
of a target.

Wheelchair Racers
Athletes who cannot walk or run race in specially designed wheelchairs. These athletes use their powerful arms to turn the wheels as quickly as they can.

ON TRACK AND FIELD

To run the fastest, to jump the highest, or to throw a javelin further than anyone else—these are some of the things that athletes train to do. There are two kinds of athletic events. In track events, athletes race each other around a track, sometimes jumping over hurdles. Field events are jumping and throwing competitions. They include high jump, javelin and shot put.

High Jump

High jumpers try to jump over a crossbar without knocking it down. The bar gets higher and higher until only the winner successfully jumps it.

Cycling through a Century

The penny-farthing was named after two British coins—the large penny and the tiny farthing. The safety bike was the first to have a chain.

penny-farthing 1870

safety bike 1879

racing cycle 1980s

Fast Riders

The first modern bicycle, with a chain linking to a wheel, appeared in 1879. Changes in design have allowed people to ride at ever-increasing speeds. Cyclists compete in long-distance road races as well as track events. The most famous road race is the Tour de France, which lasts three weeks. In track events, riders race on circular sloping tracks called velodromes.

On the Track
The sloping track in a velodrome allows riders to take corners smoothly without slowing down. In a team pursuit event there are two teams of four riders.

RIDING HORSES

Horse-riding competitions are known as equestrian events. There are three main types. In showjumping events, horses jump over obstacles such as fences and poles as they go around a fixed course. In cross-country riding, horses travel at high speed over longer courses. Dressage events display a horse's ability to move in certain ways, such as walking or trotting in circles.

Dressed for Dressage
Dressage and showjumping riders wear equestrian uniforms.

Water Obstacle

Like showjumpers, cross-country riders must take their horses across and over obstacles, such as water jumps.

In earlier times, gymnasts made leaps and somersaults over real horses! These days gymnasts perform their routines using vaulting horses, or pommel horses, which are vaulting horses with bars.

Beam
Graceful routines are performed on the long, narrow beam.

GYMNASTICS

Gymnasts need to be very strong and fit to perform their difficult routines. In a competition, judges watch gymnasts perform, then award them points for every move they do well. There are many different types of gymnastic routines, and most need special equipment. Gymnastics is a popular Olympic sport.

Rings
Gymnasts do routines such as somersaults and balances while holding on to rings.

Parallel Bars
On the parallel bars, the gymnast must swing and balance with one or both hands.

SKATING ON ICE

In cold countries, where lakes and rivers freeze over in winter, people have enjoyed skating outside for many centuries. Indoor skating rinks have existed only since the 1870s. Now, ice-skating is a popular pastime in warmer countries. Competitions between expert skaters are very athletic and exciting to watch. Ice dancers perform their graceful movements to music.

Speed Skating

Like figure skaters, speed skaters are graceful movers—but it's how fast they cover different distances that really matters.

Figure Skating

Figure skaters perform movements such as jumps and spins to music.

Downhill Dash

Downhill and slalom
skiers use ski poles to
help them as they speed
down snowy slopes.

In the Snow

Winter sports have developed from ways of getting around in the winter snow. Skiing is a popular sport, and many people ski just for fun. Top skiers compete in alpine and nordic events. Alpine events include downhill races, in which skiers dash downhill at great speed, and slalom races, in which competitors follow a course marked out by flags. Nordic events include cross-country skiing and ski-jumping.

Surfing Snow
Snowboarders ride boards like surfboards. They soar into the air from the snow to perform acrobatics.

Did You Know?

In some countries, cycling races are held in the snow! Even in the depths of winter, keen cyclists rug up to take part in long-distance road racing.

Kicking and Throwing
Tae kwon do contestants kick and punch each other, wearing helmets and padding. Judo contestants use special techniques to throw each other to the ground.

TAE KWON DO

JUDO

WARLIKE GAMES

Almost all sports are a bit like a battle, with teams or individuals trying hard to defeat each other. In fencing, people fight each other with different kinds of sword-like weapons. Modern fencers do not try to injure each other. They strike each other with the points of their weapons, but masks and padding protect them.

Kendo

Japanese samurai warriors fought fierce battles with large metal swords. Kendo is a modern version of these fights. Contestants battle it out with long bamboo swords.

A canoe is an open boat. It is paddled by one or more people using single-blade oars. A kayak is a covered boat, usually for one person. Kayaks are paddled with an oar that has a blade at each end.

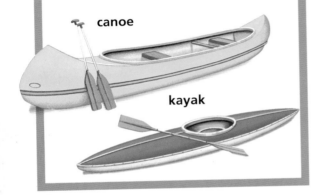

canoe

kayak

Rafting

White-water rafters travel in inflated rubber dinghies.

Rowing Team

This racing craft is designed to move swiftly through still, calm water.

ON THE WATER

The very first boats were hollow tree trunks. People later learned to make boats out of timber and animal hides, and to paddle them with shaped sticks or oars. Modern sporting craft are made of light and strong materials, such as plywood, fibreglass, aluminium, or even rubber.

Extreme Sports
Kayak racing over a white-water course tests the competitor's ability to control the craft.

Surf and Sea

Just over 200 years ago, visitors from Europe went to the islands of the Pacific Ocean and saw young men riding the waves on long, narrow, wooden boards. Today, surfboard riding and windsurfing are popular sports in many countries where there are beaches with plenty of surf.

Body Boards

Surfboard riders stand up on their boards and balance as they surf. Body boarders, however, lie flat on their boards as they catch the waves that sweep them towards the beach.

Wind Power

A sailboard is like a surfboard with a mast and sail. The rider stands and moves the sail to catch the wind. Sailboards can surf the waves or skim along on calmer waters.

Swimming Strokes

There are four main types
of swimming races. Each
has a different kind of
movement, or stroke.

backstroke

breaststroke

DIVING IN

At the start of most swimming races, competitors dive into a pool from high starting blocks. Divers jump into deep water from even higher springboards and towers. Expert divers can perform somersaults and other graceful routines on their way down. As they near the water they stretch out their arms to make as little splash as possible.

butterfly

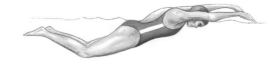

freestyle

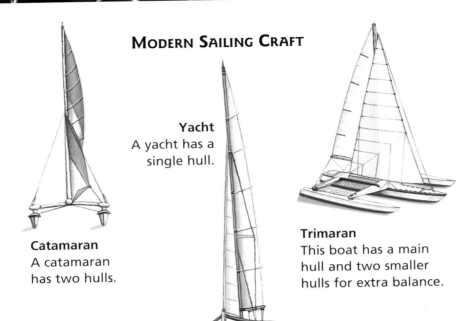

MODERN SAILING CRAFT

Yacht
A yacht has a single hull.

Catamaran
A catamaran has two hulls.

Trimaran
This boat has a main hull and two smaller hulls for extra balance.

UNDER SAIL

Until steamships were invented, people travelled across oceans in sailing ships, driven by the wind. Today, people use sailing boats for racing, or just for the fun of sailing. There are many different kinds of sailing craft. Some, like the maxi-yacht on the right, are designed to battle rough seas and high winds in long-distance ocean races.

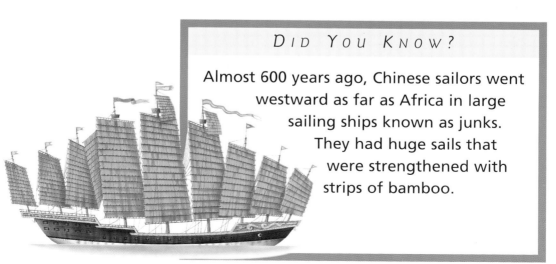

DID YOU KNOW?

Almost 600 years ago, Chinese sailors went westward as far as Africa in large sailing ships known as junks. They had huge sails that were strengthened with strips of bamboo.

GLOSSARY

dressage A horseriding event in which the horse and rider perform a series of set routines in a fairly small area.

javelin A long pole shaped like a spear. In a javelin competition the winner is the contestant who throws the javelin the furthest.

routine A series of movements that a gymnast or a diver performs in a competition.

shot put A field event in which contestants throw a heavy metal ball, called a shot, as far as possible.

stroke The kind of movements a swimmer uses to move through the water.

white water Water that is churned into a white froth as it flows quickly over rocks or rapids.

INDEX

archery	6–7
athletics	8–9
bicycles	10
bows and arrows	6
canoeing	22–23
cycling	10–11
diving	26–27
fencing	20–21
gymnastics	14–15
horse racing	4
horse riding	12–13
ice-skating	16–17
martial arts	20–21
rowing	22–23
sailing	28–29
skiing	18–19
snowboarding	18–19
surfing	24–25
swimming	26–27
wheelchair racers	8

CREDITS AND NOTES

Picture and Illustration Credits
[t=top, b=bottom, l=left, r=right, c=centre, F=front, B=back, C=cover, bg=background]
Ad-Libitum/Stuart Bowey 6tc (Benson Archery, Sydney), 6tc (Benson Archery, Sydney), 19br. **ALLSPORT** 11bl (Matthew Stockman), 15bl (Doug Pensinger), 26c (Simon Brut). **Paul Bachem** 5tc. **Corel Corporation** 1c, 7bc, 8tl, 9tl, 12bl, 13tr, 14tc, 15tr, 17tr, 17cr, 18tc, 18br, 22bc, 22cr, 23br, 25br, 29tc, 24–25cl, 30br, 4–32 borders, FCtr, Cbg. **Tony Gibbons/Bernard Thornton Artists UK** 29bl. **Ray Grinaway** 3tr, 22cl, 26bl, 26br, 27br, 27bl, 28tl, 28tc, 28tr, 31tr. **Christa Hook/Bernard Thornton Artists UK** 4bc, 5br, 20tr, 20tl, 20–21rc, BC. **Gillian Jenkins** 10tl, 10tc, 10tr. **Janet Jones** 8–9cr, 16–17bl, FCb. **Matthew Ottley** 12–13cr. **The Photo Library, Sydney** 25tr, 27tl (Tony Stone). **Oliver Rennert** 21tr. **John Richards** 2l, 6–7rc, 10c, 11br, FCtl. **Vandystadt Agence De Presse** 14c.

Acknowledgements
Weldon Owen would like to thank the following people for their assistance in the production of this book:
Jocelyne Best, Peta Gorman, Tracey Jackson, Andrew Kelly, Sarah Mattern, Emily Wood.